ELEVATING THE
GUARD

A Path To Excellence For Security Officers

WORKBOOK

ISSAC OKAFOR

Chapter 1: Introduction to Ethics in Security

Worksheet: Embracing Ethics in Security

Section 1: Understanding Ethics

1. **Reflect on Ethics:**
   - What does it mean to act ethically in your own words?
   - Why is ethical behavior crucial in the security field?

   Your thoughts:

   _____

   _____

   _____

2. **Real-Life Scenario:**
   - Think about a time when you faced an ethical dilemma. How did you handle it? What was the outcome?

   Describe the scenario:

   _____

   _____

   _____

Section 2: Code of Ethics for Security Officers

1. **Integrity and Honesty:**
   - Define what integrity means to you in your role as a security officer.
   - Provide an example of a situation where integrity guided your actions.

   Your definition:

   _____

   _____

   Your example:

   _____

   _____

2. **Respect and Fairness:**
   - How can you ensure fairness and respect in your daily duties?
   - Share a scenario where treating someone with respect made a difference.

   Your approach:

   _____

Your scenario:

_____

_____

_____

3. **Confidentiality:**
   - o   Why is confidentiality important in your role?
   - o   List three ways you can protect sensitive information.

   Your explanation:

   _____

   _____

   Three ways:

   - o   _____
   - o   _____
   - o   _____

4. **Professionalism:**
   - o   What does professionalism mean to you in the context of security?
   - o   Describe how you demonstrate professionalism at work.

   Your meaning:

   _____

   _____

   Your demonstration:

   _____

   _____

_____

Section 3: Benefits of Ethical Adherence

1. **Trust and Credibility:**
   1. How do ethical actions build trust with the public?
   2. Provide an example where your ethical behavior enhanced credibility.

   Building trust:

   _____

   _____

   Your example:

   _____

   _____

2. **Professional Growth:**
    1. How can adherence to ethics influence your career advancement?
    2. Share a personal story of how ethics have positively impacted your career.

Influence on career:

_____

_____

Your story:

_____

_____

3. **Legal Issues Prevention:**
    1. Why is ethical behavior crucial for avoiding legal problems?
    2. Identify three potential legal issues that can arise from unethical conduct.

Importance:

_____

_____

Three issues:

    1. _____

    2. _____

    3. _____

Section 4: The Security Officer's Pledge

1. **Craft Your Pledge:**
    1. Write your own pledge based on the principles of integrity, fairness, confidentiality, professionalism, and service to the community.

Your pledge:

_____

_____

_____

2. **Daily Commitment:**
    1. How will you ensure that you live by this pledge every day? List three actionable steps.

Three steps:

    1. _____

    2. _____

    3. _____

Section 5: Core Virtues

1. **Integrity:**
   - Reflect on a time when your integrity was tested. How did you respond?

   Your reflection:

   _____

   _____

2. **Vigilance:**
   - What does vigilance mean to you? How do you maintain vigilance in your role?

   Your meaning:

   _____

   _____

   Maintaining vigilance:

   _____

   _____

3. **Compassion:**
   - Share an instance where compassion played a key role in your duties.

   Your instance:

   _____

   _____

4. **Courage:**
   - Describe a situation where you had to show courage in your role

   Your situation:

   _____

   _____

5. **Accountability:**
   - Why is accountability important in security work? How do you practice accountability?

   Importance:

   _____

   _____

   Your practice:

   _____

   _____

<u>Section 6: Ethical Dilemmas</u>

1. **Privacy vs. Security:**
   - ○ How would you handle a situation where you must balance privacy and security?

   Your approach:

   _____

   _____

2. **Conflict of Interest:**
   - ○ What steps will you take to avoid conflicts of interest in your role?

   Your steps:

   _____

   _____

3. **Use of Force:**
   - ○ Describe your thought process in deciding the appropriate use of force.

   Your thought process:

   _____

   _____

Section 7: Conclusion

1. **Reflect on Learning:**
   - ○ Summarize the key takeaways from this chapter on ethics.
   - ○ How will you apply these lessons in your daily work?

   Key takeaways:

   _____

   _____

   Application:

   _____

   _____

This worksheet aims to reinforce the importance of ethics in the security profession, helping you to reflect on your own practices and commit to upholding the highest standards in your role. Embrace these principles, and let them guide you to become a beacon of integrity and professionalism in your field.

Chapter 2: The Role of a Security Officer

Worksheet: Embracing Your Role as a Security Officer

Section 1: General Duties of a Security Officer

1. **Daily Responsibilities:**
   - List three general duties of a security officer.
   - Describe how each duty contributes to overall safety.

   Duties:

   - _____
   - _____
   - _____

   Contributions to Safety:

   - _____
   - _____
   - _____

2. **Emergency Readiness:**
   - What are three key actions you must take during an emergency?
   - How can you prepare yourself to handle emergencies effectively?

   Key Actions:

   - _____
   - _____
   - _____

   Preparation Strategies:

   _____
   _____
   _____

3. **Reporting:**
   - Why is writing detailed reports important?
   - Provide an example of an incident where a detailed report could prevent future issues.

   Importance of Reports:

   _____
   _____

Example Incident:

_____

_____

_____

Section 2: Specific Duties

1. **Patrolling:**
   - Describe the importance of patrolling specific areas.
   - Share a scenario where your presence during a patrol prevented an issue.

   Importance of Patrolling:

   _____

   _____

   Scenario:

   _____

   _____

2. **Monitoring Cameras:**
   - How does monitoring security cameras enhance your effectiveness?
   - Describe a situation where camera surveillance helped you respond quickly to an issue.

   Effectiveness of Monitoring:

   _____

   _____

   Situation:

   _____

   _____

3. **Checking Identification:**
   - Why is checking identification critical in certain locations?
   - How do you ensure you handle this duty professionally and efficiently?

   Importance of Checking IDs:

   _____

   _____

   Professional Handling:

   _____

   _____

Section 3: Public Relations

1. **Effective Communication:**
   - Why is good communication essential for a security officer?
   - Provide an example of how clear communication helped you resolve a situation.

   Importance of Communication:

   _____
   _____

   Example:

   _____
   _____

2. **Building Trust:**
   - How can being friendly and helpful build trust with the public?
   - Describe a time when your positive interaction made a difference.

   Building Trust:

   _____
   _____

   Positive Interaction:

   _____
   _____

3. **Handling Complaints:**
   - What steps do you take to handle complaints effectively?
   - Share an instance where resolving a complaint improved the situation.

   Steps for Handling Complaints:

   _____
   _____

   Instance:

   _____
   _____

Section 4: Theft Prevention

1. **Visible Presence:**
   - How does being visible help in preventing theft?
   - Describe a scenario where your visible presence deterred a potential thief.

   Importance of Visibility:

   _____
   _____

Scenario:

_____

_____

2. **Using Technology:**
   - List three ways technology aids in theft prevention.
   - Explain how you utilize these technologies in your daily duties.

   Ways Technology Helps:

   - _____
   - _____
   - _____

   Utilization in Duties:

   _____

   _____

3. **Training Staff:**
   - Why is training other staff members on theft prevention important?
   - How do you conduct a training session effectively?

   Importance of Training:

   _____

   _____

   Effective Training:

   _____

   _____

_____

Section 5: Employee Theft

1. **Identifying Signs:**
   1. What are three common signs of employee theft?
   2. How would you approach investigating these signs?

   Common Signs:

   3. _____
   4. _____
   5. _____

   Approach to Investigation:

   _____

   _____

2. **Prevention Strategies:**
    1. List two strategies to prevent employee theft.
    2. How do these strategies help maintain a secure environment?

Prevention Strategies:

_____

_____

Maintaining Security:

_____

_____

_____

Section 6: Reflection and Growth

1. **Daily Challenges:**
    - What are the top three challenges you face as a security officer?
    - How do you overcome these challenges?

Challenges:

- _____
- _____
- _____

Overcoming Challenges:

_____

_____

2. **Continuous Learning:**
    - Why is continuous learning important in your role?
    - What steps will you take to stay updated with the latest security practices?

Importance of Learning:

_____

_____

Steps for Staying Updated:

_____

_____

This worksheet is designed to help you reflect on and embrace the various aspects of your role as a security officer. By understanding your duties, improving your public relations skills, and staying vigilant in theft prevention, you can enhance your effectiveness and make a significant impact on the safety and security of your environment.

Chapter 3: Nationwide Suspicious Activity Reporting

Worksheet: Enhancing Community Safety through SAR

Section 1: Understanding Suspicious Activity Reporting

1. **Defining Suspicious Activity:**
   - What qualifies as suspicious activity in your own words?
   - Provide an example of suspicious activity you might encounter in your role.

   Your definition:

   _____

   _____

   Example:

   _____

   _____

2. **Importance of Reporting:**
   - Why is it crucial to report suspicious activities?
   - How can SAR prevent potential threats?

   Importance:

   _____

   Prevention:

   _____

   _____

3. **Privacy Considerations:**
   - How should you ensure your SAR focuses on behavior rather than personal characteristics?
   - Provide an example of an objective, behavior-focused report.

   Ensuring Focus on Behavior:

   _____

   _____

   Example Report:

   _____

   _____

Section 2: Role of Security Professionals in SAR

1. **Vigilance:**
   - Describe what it means to be vigilant as a security officer.
   - Share a time when your vigilance helped identify a potential threat.

   Description:

   _____

   _____

   Example:

   _____

   _____

2. **Assessing Situations:**
   - What steps do you take to assess the risk level of a suspicious activity?
   - Provide an example where your assessment prevented a potential incident.

   Steps:

   _____

   _____

   Example:

   _____

   _____

3. **Reporting Protocols:**
   - Outline the protocols for reporting suspicious activities in your organization.
   - Why is it important to follow these protocols precisely?

   Protocols:

   _____

   _____

   Importance:

   _____

   _____

Section 3: Becoming the Eyes and Ears of Companies and the Community

1. **Building Awareness:**
   - How do you stay aware of what's normal in your environment?
   - Share a situation where your awareness helped identify something unusual.

   Staying Aware:

   _____

   _____

Situation:

_____

_____

2. **Community Connection:**
   - ○ How does building a connection with the community enhance your effectiveness?
   - ○ Provide an example of how your relationship with the community helped in SAR.

Enhancing Effectiveness:

_____

_____

Example:

_____

_____

3. **Quick Response:**
   - ○ Why is quick response crucial in suspicious activity reporting?
   - ○ Describe a scenario where your quick response made a difference.

Importance of Quick Response:

_____

_____

Scenario:

_____

_____

Section 4: 'See Something, Say Something' Campaign

1. **Understanding the Campaign:**
   - ○ What is the main message of the "See Something, Say Something" campaign?
   - ○ How does this campaign impact community safety?

Main Message:

_____

_____

Impact on Safety:

_____

_____

2. **Encouraging Reports:**
   - ○ How can you encourage others to report suspicious activities?
   - ○ Share a time when you encouraged someone to report, and it led to a positive outcome.

Encouraging Others:

_____

_____

Positive Outcome:

_____

_____

3. **Handling Reports:**
   - What steps do you take to ensure reports are handled properly?
   - Why is it important to treat every report seriously?

Steps:

_____

_____

Importance:

_____

_____

_____

Section 5: Reflection and Growth

1. **Learning from Experience:**
   - Reflect on a time when your SAR efforts made a significant impact.
   - How did this experience influence your approach to SAR?

Reflection:

_____

_____

Influence:

_____

_____

2. **Continuous Improvement:**
   - Why is continuous training important for effective SAR?
   - What steps will you take to improve your SAR skills?

Importance of Training:

_____

_____

Steps for Improvement:

_____

_____

_____

This worksheet aims to enhance your understanding and implementation of Suspicious Activity Reporting. By recognizing and reporting suspicious activities, you contribute significantly to the safety and security of your community. Stay vigilant, stay informed, and remember: your proactive efforts make a difference.

Chapter 4: Report Writing

Worksheet: Mastering the Art of Report Writing

Section 1: Purposes of a Report

1. **Documenting Incidents:**
   - Describe a recent incident you had to document.
   - How did your report help in recalling and understanding the event?

   Incident Description:
   _____
   _____

   Report's Impact:
   _____
   _____

2. **Legal Evidence:**
   - Why is it important for reports to be clear and factual for legal purposes?
   - Provide an example of how a well-written report could influence a legal case.

   Importance:
   _____
   _____

   Example:
   _____
   _____

3. **Communication Tool:**
   - How does your report serve as a communication bridge between different parties?
   - Share an instance where your report streamlined responses or decisions.

   Communication Role:
   _____
   _____

   Instance:
   _____
   _____

4. **Accountability:**
   - How does report writing demonstrate your accountability as a security officer?
   - Describe a situation where your report highlighted your responsibility.

Accountability:

_____

_____

Situation:

_____

_____

5. **Improving Security:**
   - How can reports help in improving security measures?
   - Give an example of a pattern or repeated issue identified through reports.

Improvement Role:

_____

_____

Example:

_____

_____

6. **Training and Learning:**
   - How can reports serve as training tools for new security officers?
   - Share a report that you believe is a good learning example and explain why.

Training Role:

_____

_____

Example Report:

_____

_____

Section 2: Types of Reports

1. **Incident Reports:**
   - What key details should be included in an incident report?
   - Write a brief incident report based on a hypothetical situation.

Key Details:

_____

_____

Hypothetical Incident Report:

_____

_____

2. **Daily Activity Reports:**
   - Why are daily activity reports essential?

       ○   Provide an example of a typical daily activity report entry.

Importance:

_____

_____

Example Entry:

_____

_____

3. **Emergency Situation Reports:**
   - ○ What information is critical in an emergency situation report?
   - ○ Describe an emergency scenario and how you would report it.

Critical Information:

_____

_____

Emergency Scenario:

_____

_____

4. **Visitor Logs:**
   - ○ What details are necessary in a visitor log?
   - ○ Create a sample entry for a visitor log.

Necessary Details:

_____

_____

Sample Entry:

_____

_____

5. **Maintenance Reports:**
   - ○ How should you document a maintenance issue in a report?
   - ○ Write a brief maintenance report for a hypothetical issue.

Documentation Approach:

_____

_____

Hypothetical Maintenance Report:

_____

_____

6. **Shift Handover Reports:**
   - ○ What should be included in a shift handover report?
   - ○ Draft a sample shift handover report entry.

Inclusions:

_____

_____

Sample Entry:

_____

_____

_____

Section 3: Who Reads the Report You Write?

1. **Security Management:**
   - What information is most relevant to security management in your reports?
   - Provide an example of a report entry tailored for management.

   Relevant Information:

   _____

   _____

   Example Entry:

   _____

   _____

2. **Law Enforcement:**
   - How should you structure your report to assist law enforcement?
   - Write a report entry that would be useful for law enforcement officers.

   Structure Tips:

   _____

   _____

   Example Entry:

   _____

   _____

3. **Legal Teams:**
   - What are the key elements that legal teams look for in a report?
   - Create a sample report entry that meets these criteria.

   Key Elements:

   _____

   _____

   Sample Entry:

   _____

   _____

4. **Company Executives:**
   - How can you present information concisely for company executives?

o   Draft a brief report entry suitable for executive review.

Concise Presentation:

_____

_____

Sample Entry:

_____

_____

5. **Other Staff:**
   o   What specific information might other staff members need from your reports?
   o   Provide an example of a report entry tailored for another department.

Specific Information:

_____

_____

Example Entry:

_____

_____

6. **Insurance Companies:**
   o   What details are critical for insurance companies in incident reports?
   o   Write a sample report entry focused on insurance requirements.

Critical Details:

_____

_____

Sample Entry:

_____

_____

Section 4: The Building Blocks of Report Writing

1. **Who:**
   o   List the types of individuals you need to identify in your reports.
   o   Provide an example description for each type.

Types:

_____

_____

Example Descriptions:

_____

_____

2. **What:**
   - ○ What key details should you include when describing the incident?
   - ○ Write a detailed description of a hypothetical incident.

   Key Details:

   _____

   _____

   Hypothetical Description:

   _____

   _____

3. **Where:**
   - ○ How should you document the location of an incident?
   - ○ Provide a sample location description.

   Documentation Tips:

   _____

   _____

   Sample Description:

   _____

   _____

4. **When:**
   - ○ Why is precise timing important in your reports?
   - ○ Create a timeline for a hypothetical incident.

   Importance of Timing:

   _____

   _____

   Hypothetical Timeline:

   _____

   _____

5. **Why:**
   - ○ How can you document the motives or reasons behind an incident?
   - ○ Write a brief explanation for a hypothetical incident.

   Documentation Tips:

   _____

   _____

   Hypothetical Explanation:

   _____

   _____

6. **How:**
   - ○ What steps should you include to detail how the incident occurred?

       o   Provide a step-by-step account of a hypothetical incident.

Steps:

_____

_____

Step-by-Step Account:

_____

_____

_____

Section 5: Common Problems in Report Writing

1. **Vagueness:**
    - o   How can you avoid being vague in your reports?
    - o   Rewrite a vague report entry to make it specific.

Avoiding Vagueness:

_____

_____

Original Entry:

_____

_____

Rewritten Entry:

_____

_____

_____

2. **Bias:**
    - o   How can you ensure your reports remain unbiased?
    - o   Provide an example of an unbiased report entry.

Ensuring Objectivity:

_____

_____

Example Entry:

_____

_____

3. **Grammatical Errors:**
    - o   What steps can you take to avoid grammatical errors in your reports?
    - o   Proofread a sample report entry and correct any errors.

Avoiding Errors:

_____

_____

Sample Entry:

Corrected Entry:

_____
_____
_____

4. **Too Much Information:**
   - ○ How do you ensure your reports are concise and relevant?
   - ○ Edit a sample report entry to remove unnecessary details.

Ensuring Conciseness:

_____
_____

Original Entry:

_____
_____

Edited Entry:

_____
_____

5. **Repetition:**
   - ○ How can you avoid repetition in your reports?
   - ○ Rewrite a repetitive report entry to be more concise.

Avoiding Repetition:

_____
_____

Original Entry:

_____
_____

Rewritten Entry:

_____
_____

This worksheet provides a hands-on approach to mastering report writing, an essential skill for security officers. By guiding users through real-world scenarios and structured exercises, the workbook enhances their ability to produce clear, factual, and relevant reports that serve multiple purposes—from legal documentation to communication across departments. The fillable sections allow officers to practice specific report types, understand audience needs, and refine their writing style to improve accuracy, professionalism, and accountability in their reporting.

Chapter 5: Managing Bomb Threats

Worksheet: Managing Bomb Threats

Introduction: Bomb Threat and Incident Response Management

Scenario Reflection:

- Imagine you are at your post and receive a bomb threat. Describe your immediate feelings and thoughts.
  Your Reflection:
  _____

  _____

- Why is it important to be prepared and decisive in such situations?
  Importance:
  _____

  _____

  _____

Section 1: Understanding Common Methods of Making Bomb Threats

1. **Telephone Calls:**
   - What steps should you take if you receive a bomb threat via telephone?
     Steps:
     _____

     _____

   - How can you gather useful information from the caller?
     Information Gathering:
     _____

     _____

2. **Email and Electronic Messages:**
   - What should you do upon receiving a bomb threat via email?
     Actions:
     _____

     _____

   - What details should you look for to assess the threat's credibility?
     Details:
     _____

     _____

3. **Social Media Platforms:**
   - How can you effectively monitor and respond to bomb threats made on social media?
     Monitoring and Response:

4. **Written Notes or Letters:**
   o Describe the steps you should take when you find a bomb threat in written form.
   Steps:

5. **Symbolic or Indirect Threats:**
   o How should you handle an unattended package that might be a bomb threat?
   Handling Unattended Package:

Section 2: Pre-Planning

1. **Understanding the Facility:**
   o List the critical areas you need to be familiar with in your facility.
   Critical Areas:

2. **Establishing Communication Channels:**
   o What are the essential communication lines you need to establish?
   Communication Lines:

3. **Evacuation Plans:**
   o Outline the key components of an effective evacuation plan.
   Evacuation Plan Components:

4. **Threat Assessment Protocols:**
   o Describe the criteria for assessing the credibility of a bomb threat.
   Assessment Criteria:

5. **Training and Education:**
   o Why is regular training essential for bomb threat management?
   Importance of Training:

6. **Equipment Readiness:**
   o List the equipment that needs to be ready for a bomb threat response.
   Equipment:

_____

_____

_____

Section 3: Bomb Management Personnel

1. **Roles and Responsibilities:**
   - What are the key roles and responsibilities of each team member in managing a bomb threat?
     Security Officers:

     _____

     _____

     Bomb Squad:

     _____

     _____

     Emergency Services:

     _____

     _____

     Facility Management:

     _____

     _____

     Communication Center:

     _____

     _____

     Administrative Staff:

     _____

     _____

_____

Section 4: Reasons for Bomb Threats

1. **Motivations:**
   - Identify and describe the common motivations behind bomb threats.
     Criminal Intent:

     _____

     _____

     Political or Ideological Reasons:

     _____

     _____

     Personal Vendettas:

     _____

     _____

     Mental Health Issues:

Pranks or Hoaxes:

_____

_____

Attention Seeking:

_____

_____

Section 5: Evaluating the Threat and Making Decisions

1. **Initial Assessment:**
   - What factors should you consider in the initial assessment of a bomb threat?
   Assessment Factors:

   _____

   _____

2. **Information Gathering:**
   - How can you effectively gather information about the threat?
   Information Gathering:

   _____

   _____

3. **Consulting with Experts:**
   - Why is it important to involve experts in the assessment process?
   Importance:

   _____

   _____

4. **Decision to Evacuate:**
   - What criteria should you use to decide whether to evacuate?
   Evacuation Criteria:

   _____

   _____

5. **Communication Strategy:**
   - Outline the steps for effective communication during a bomb threat.
   Communication Steps:

   _____

   _____

6. **Post-Threat Evaluation:**
   - What should be included in the post-threat evaluation process?
   Evaluation Components:

   _____

   _____

Section 6: Unattended vs. Suspicious Package Response

1. **Unattended Packages:**
   - How should you assess and handle an unattended package?
   Assessment and Handling:

   _____

   _____

2. **Suspicious Packages:**
   - What steps should you take when you encounter a suspicious package?
   Steps:

   _____

   _____

3. **Practical Examples:**
   - Provide a detailed response for handling an unattended package and a suspicious package in your facility.
   Unattended Package Example:

   _____

   _____

   Suspicious Package Example:

   _____

   _____

Section 7: Search Techniques

1. **Visual Inspection:**
   - Describe the process of conducting a visual inspection for potential threats.
   Visual Inspection Process:

   _____

   _____

2. **Systematic Search Techniques:**
   - Explain the grid and zonal search methods.
   Grid Search:

   _____

   _____

   Zonal Search:

   _____

   _____

3. **Use of Specialized Equipment:**
   - List the specialized equipment used in bomb threat searches and their purposes.
   Equipment:

   _____

   _____

4. **Avoiding Disturbance:**

- What precautions should you take to avoid disturbing a suspicious item?
  Precautions:
  _____
  _____

5. **Searching High and Low:**
   - How should you conduct searches in high and low areas?
     High Areas:
     _____
     _____

     Low Areas:
     _____
     _____

6. **Communication:**
   - Why is communication important during a search, and how should it be maintained?
     Communication Importance:
     _____
     _____

     Maintenance:
     _____
     _____

7. **Safety Precautions:**
   - What safety precautions should you take during a bomb threat search?
     Safety Precautions:
     _____
     _____

Section 8: Organized Search Methods

1. **Coordination with the Bomb Squad:**
   - How can you effectively coordinate with the bomb squad during a search?
     Coordination Steps:
     _____
     _____

2. **Initial Security Officer Role:**
   - What are the initial responsibilities of security officers before the bomb squad arrives?
     Initial Responsibilities:
     _____
     _____

3. **Dividing the Search Area:**
   - Explain how to divide the search area for an organized search.
     Search Area Division:

4. **Methodical Search:**
   - Describe the key practices for conducting a methodical search.
   Key Practices:

5. **Evacuation and Access Control:**
   - What are the steps for managing evacuation and access control during a bomb threat?
   Evacuation and Access Control:

6. **Documentation:**
   - What should be documented during and after a bomb threat search?
   Documentation:

7. **Post-Search Debrief:**
   - Outline the components of an effective post-search debrief.
   Debrief Components:

Section 9: Key Takeaways and Final Reflection

1. **Reflection on Pre-Planning:**
   - Why is pre-planning critical in bomb threat management?
   Reflection:

2. **Roles and Responsibilities:**
   - How do clearly defined roles and responsibilities enhance bomb threat management?
   Enhancements:

3. **Evaluating Threats:**
   - What are the key steps in evaluating the credibility of a bomb threat?
   Key Steps:

4. **Handling Packages:**

    o How should you distinguish between and handle unattended and suspicious packages?

    Distinguishing and Handling:

_____

_____

5. **Search Techniques:**
   - o Summarize the importance of systematic search techniques in bomb threat response.

   Summary:

_____

_____

6. **Organized Search Methods:**
   - o What are the benefits of using organized search methods?

   Benefits:

_____

_____

7. **Continuous Improvement:**
   - o How can continuous improvement practices enhance your bomb threat management capabilities?

   Enhancement:

_____

_____

_____

<u>Final Reflection:</u>

- Reflect on your current bomb threat management practices. What areas do you feel confident in, and where do you see room for improvement?

  Your Reflection:

_____

_____

- How will you apply the principles learned in this chapter to enhance your preparedness and response to bomb threats?

  Application of Principles:

_____

_____

This worksheet is designed to help you internalize and apply the key concepts of managing bomb threats. Regular practice and reflection on these principles will ensure that you are well-prepared to handle these critical situations effectively.

Chapter 6: Fire Safety

Worksheet: Fire Safety for Security Officers

Section 1: Overview

Fire Safety Basics

1. **Identify Fire Hazards:**
   - List common fire hazards you might find in your workplace.
     - Overloaded electrical outlets
     - Flammable materials improperly stored
     - Blocked escape routes
   - What steps can you take to mitigate these hazards?
     Steps:

     _____

     _____

2. **Fire Detection Systems:**
   - Why is regular maintenance and testing of fire detection systems important?
     Importance:

     _____

     _____

3. **Evacuation Procedures:**
   - Describe the components of an effective evacuation plan.
     - Clear signage
     - Well-lit escape routes
     - Regular fire drills
   - *Components:*

     _____

     _____

4. **Legal and Ethical Responsibilities:**
   - Why is it important to adhere to local fire codes and conduct regular safety checks?
     Importance:

     _____

     _____

5. **Impact on Business and Community:**
   - How can fires affect businesses and communities beyond immediate physical damage?
     Impact:

     _____

     _____

6. **Proactive Measures:**

○ What proactive measures can you take to enhance fire safety?
Measures:

_____

_____

7. **Real-World Scenario:**
   ○ Describe a scenario where proactive fire safety measures prevented a disaster.
   Scenario:

   _____

   _____

_____

Section 2: Fire Chemistry

Understanding Fire Chemistry

1. **Elements of Fire:**
   ○ Explain the fire triangle: heat, fuel, and oxygen.
   Explanation:

   _____

   _____

2. **Heat Sources:**
   ○ List potential heat sources in your workplace.
   Sources:

   _____

   _____

3. **Fuel Types:**
   ○ Identify various types of fuel that can cause fires.
   Types of Fuel:

   _____

   _____

4. **Oxygen:**
   ○ Why is controlling oxygen important in fire suppression?
   Importance:

   _____

   _____

5. **Fire Tetrahedron:**
   ○ Describe the fire tetrahedron and its significance in complex fire scenarios.
   Description:

   _____

   _____

6. **Practical Example:**
   ○ Provide a real-world example of fire chemistry in action.
   Example:

_____

_____

_____

<u>Section 3: Classes of Fire</u>

Different Types of Fires

1. **Class A:**
   - Describe Class A fires and the appropriate extinguishing methods.
     Description:

   _____

   _____

2. **Class B:**
   - Describe Class B fires and the appropriate extinguishing methods.
     Description:

   _____

   _____

3. **Class C:**
   - Describe Class C fires and the appropriate extinguishing methods.
     Description:

   _____

   _____

4. **Class D:**
   - Describe Class D fires and the appropriate extinguishing methods.
     Description:

   _____

   _____

5. **Class K:**
   - Describe Class K fires and the appropriate extinguishing methods.
     Description:

   _____

   _____

6. **Research Insights:**
   - Summarize key research findings on fire extinguishers and fire classes.
     Summary:

   _____

   _____

_____

<u>Section 4: Hazardous Materials</u>

Managing Hazardous Materials

1. **Storage and Handling:**
   - What are the best practices for storing and handling hazardous materials?
   Best Practices:

   _____

   _____

2. **Emergency Response:**
   - What steps should you take in the event of a fire involving hazardous materials?
   Steps:

   _____

   _____

3. **Material Safety Data Sheets (MSDS):**
   - Why are MSDS important and how should they be used?
   Importance and Use:

   _____

   _____

4. **Training and Awareness:**
   - How can you ensure all personnel are trained and aware of hazardous material risks?
   Training and Awareness:

   _____

   _____

5. **Preventive Measures:**
   - List preventive measures to manage hazardous materials safely.
   Measures:

   _____

   _____

6. **Real-World Scenario:**
   - Describe a scenario where proper management of hazardous materials prevented a fire.
   Scenario:

   _____

   _____

Section 5: Types of Fire Extinguishers

Using Fire Extinguishers

1. **Water Extinguishers:**
   - When should you use a water extinguisher?
   Usage:

   _____

   _____

2. **Foam Extinguishers:**

- When should you use a foam extinguisher?
    Usage:

    _____

    _____

3. **Dry Chemical Extinguishers:**
    - When should you use a dry chemical extinguisher?
    Usage:

    _____

    _____

4. **Carbon Dioxide (CO2) Extinguishers:**
    - When should you use a CO2 extinguisher?
    Usage:

    _____

    _____

5. **Wet Chemical Extinguishers:**
    - When should you use a wet chemical extinguisher?
    Usage:

    _____

    _____

6. **Dry Powder Extinguishers:**
    - When should you use a dry powder extinguisher?
    Usage:

    _____

    _____

7. **PASS Technique:**
    - Describe the PASS technique for using a fire extinguisher.
    Technique:

    _____

    _____

8. **Research Insights:**
    - Summarize key research findings on the effectiveness of different fire extinguishers.
    Summary:

    _____

    _____

9. **Training and Familiarization:**
    - How can you ensure everyone is trained and familiar with the different types of fire extinguishers?
    Training and Familiarization:

    _____

    _____

Section 6: Extinguishing Small Fires

Steps to Extinguish Small Fires

1. **Assessment:**
   - How do you assess the size and type of a fire?
   Assessment:

   _____

   _____

2. **Choosing the Right Extinguisher:**
   - How do you choose the right extinguisher based on the fire type?
   Choice:

   _____

   _____

3. **Using the Extinguisher:**
   - Explain the steps of the PASS technique.
   Steps:

   _____

   _____

4. **Ensuring Safety:**
   - What safety measures should you take while extinguishing a fire?
   Safety Measures:

   _____

   _____

5. **After Extinguishing:**
   - What steps should you take after the fire is extinguished?
   Post-Extinguishing Steps:

   _____

   _____

6. **Real-World Scenario:**
   - Describe a scenario where you successfully extinguished a small fire.
   Scenario:

   _____

   _____

Section 7: Your Safety

Prioritizing Your Safety

1. **Risk Evaluation:**
   - How do you evaluate the risks involved in a fire situation?
   Evaluation:

2. **Protective Equipment:**
   - What protective equipment should you use during a fire?
   Equipment:

   _____

   _____

3. **Smoke Awareness:**
   - How can you protect yourself from smoke inhalation?
   Protection:

   _____

   _____

4. **Heat and Fire Behavior:**
   - What signs should you look for regarding fire spread and structural weakness?
   Signs:

   _____

   _____

5. **Post-Incident Care:**
   - What steps should you take for post-incident care and debriefing?
   Post-Incident Care:

   _____

   _____

6. **Real-World Scenario:**
   - Describe a scenario where you prioritized your safety during a fire.
   Scenario:

   _____

   _____

Conclusion

Reflecting on Fire Safety

1. **Preparedness:**
   - How can you ensure you are always prepared for a fire emergency?
   Preparedness:

   _____

   _____

2. **Proactive Measures:**
   - What proactive measures will you implement to enhance fire safety?
   Measures:

   _____

   _____

3. **Emergency Response:**

     o How will you improve your emergency response and evacuation plans?
         Improvements:

_____

_____

4. **Training and Awareness:**
   o How will you ensure continuous training and awareness for fire safety?
   Training and Awareness:

_____

_____

5. **Collaboration with Emergency Services:**
   o How can you collaborate more effectively with local fire departments and emergency services?
   Collaboration:

_____

_____

6. **Continuous Learning and Adaptation:**
   o How will you stay updated with the latest fire safety standards and technologies?
   Learning and Adaptation:

_____

_____

_____

This workbook is designed to help you internalize and apply the key concepts of fire safety. Regular practice, reflection, and continuous improvement will ensure that you are well-prepared to handle fire emergencies effectively.

Chapter 7: Cargo Theft and Theft Prevention

Worksheet: Cargo Theft and Theft Prevention for Security Officers

Introduction

Understanding Cargo Theft

1. **Definition and Importance:**
   - What is cargo theft and why is it a significant concern in logistics and transportation?
     Definition and Importance:

   _____

   _____

2. **Impacts of Cargo Theft:**
   - How does cargo theft affect businesses and the global supply chain?
     Impacts:

   _____

   _____

3. **Roles of Security Officers:**
   - What are the key responsibilities of security officers in preventing cargo theft?
     Responsibilities:

   _____

   _____

_____

Section 1: Definition of Cargo

Understanding Cargo

1. **What Constitutes Cargo:**
   - Define cargo in the context of security and list examples of different types of cargo.
     Definition and Examples:

   _____

   _____

2. **Transport Methods:**
   - Describe the different methods of cargo transportation and the unique security challenges each presents.
     Transport Methods and Challenges:

   _____

   _____

3. **Real-World Scenario:**

- Describe a scenario involving the transportation of high-value electronics and the security measures needed.
  Scenario:

  _____

  _____

Section 2: The Profile of a Typical Cargo Thief

Understanding Cargo Thieves

1. **Characteristics of Cargo Thieves:**
   - List common characteristics and behaviors of cargo thieves.
     Characteristics and Behaviors:

     _____

     _____

2. **Motivations:**
   - What motivates cargo thieves, and why do they target specific types of cargo?
     Motivations:

     _____

     _____

3. **Techniques and Tools:**
   - What techniques and tools do cargo thieves commonly use?
     Techniques and Tools:

     _____

     _____

4. **Real-World Example:**
   - Provide a real-world example of a cargo theft involving inside knowledge.
     Example:

     _____

     _____

Section 3: Types of Cargo Theft

Different Forms of Cargo Theft

1. **Armed Hijacking:**
   - Define armed hijacking and describe the stages involved.
     Definition and Stages:

     _____

     _____

2. **Leaking:**

- o Explain what leaking is and its impact on cargo theft.
  Explanation and Impact:

  _____

  _____

3. **Recouping:**
   - o Describe the process of recouping and how it affects cargo theft.
     Description and Effects:

     _____

     _____

4. **Fictitious Driver Pick Up:**
   - o What is fictitious driver pick up, and how can it be prevented?
     Definition and Prevention:

     _____

     _____

5. **Warehouse Burglary:**
   - o Describe how warehouse burglary occurs and the preventive measures.
     Description and Prevention:

     _____

     _____

Section 4: Tools of the Cargo Thief

Tools and Techniques

1. **Physical Tools:**
   - o List and describe common physical tools used by cargo thieves.
     Tools and Descriptions:

     _____

     _____

2. **Technological Tools:**
   - o What technological tools do cargo thieves use to disrupt security systems?
     Technological Tools:

     _____

     _____

3. **Social Engineering:**
   - o Explain how social engineering is used in cargo theft.
     Explanation:

     _____

     _____

<u>Section 5: Freights Targeted by Cargo Thieves</u>

High-Risk Cargo Types

1. **Electronics:**
   - Why are electronics a popular target for cargo thieves?
   Reasons:

   _____

   _____

2. **Pharmaceuticals:**
   - Describe the risks associated with pharmaceutical cargo theft.
   Risks:

   _____

   _____

3. **Apparel:**
   - Why is brand-name clothing targeted by cargo thieves?
   Reasons:

   _____

   _____

4. **Food and Beverages:**
   - Explain why food and beverage cargo is frequently targeted.
   Explanation:

   _____

   _____

5. **Research Insights:**
   - Summarize research findings on the impact of implementing GPS tracking on cargo theft incidents.
   Research Summary:

   _____

   _____

_____

<u>Section 6: Problems Encountered with Cargo Theft Investigation</u>

Challenges in Investigating Cargo Theft

1. **Lack of Evidence:**
   - How does the lack of evidence hinder cargo theft investigations?
   Explanation:

   _____

   _____

2. **Delayed Reporting:**
   - Describe the impact of delayed reporting on cargo theft investigations.
   Impact:

3. **Jurisdictional Issues:**
   - Explain how jurisdictional issues complicate cargo theft investigations.
   Explanation:

4. **Insider Involvement:**
   - What challenges arise when insiders are involved in cargo theft?
   Challenges:

5. **Complexity of Supply Chain:**
   - How does the complexity of the supply chain affect cargo theft investigations?
   Explanation:

6. **Technological Challenges:**
   - Describe the technological challenges in investigating cargo theft.
   Challenges:

Section 7: What Should Patrol Officers Look For

Vigilance on Patrol

1. **Suspicious Vehicles:**
   - What should patrol officers look for regarding suspicious vehicles?
   Indicators:

2. **Unusual Activity:**
   - Describe examples of unusual activity that may indicate potential cargo theft.
   Examples:

3. **Improper Identification:**
   - What are the signs of improper identification that patrol officers should watch for?
   Signs:

4. **Tampered Locks or Seals:**

- How can patrol officers identify tampered locks or seals?
  Indicators:
  _____
  _____

5. **Unsecured Cargo Areas:**
   - What constitutes an unsecured cargo area, and why is it a concern?
   Explanation:
   _____
   _____

6. **Technology Interference:**
   - How can patrol officers detect technology interference?
   Detection Methods:
   _____
   _____

_____

Section 8: How Can a Driver Lessen the Chance of Becoming a Cargo Theft Victim

Driver Strategies for Cargo Theft Prevention

1. **Stay Vigilant:**
   - What actions can drivers take to stay vigilant against cargo theft?
   Actions:
   _____
   _____

2. **Secure the Vehicle:**
   - List the steps drivers should take to secure their vehicle.
   Steps:
   _____
   _____

3. **Use Technology:**
   - How can drivers use technology to protect against cargo theft?
   Technology Uses:
   _____
   _____

4. **Plan Routes Carefully:**
   - Why is careful route planning important for drivers?
   Importance:
   _____
   _____

5. **Parking in Secure Areas:**
   - Describe the best practices for choosing secure parking areas.
   Best Practices:

6. **Avoid Discussing Cargo:**
   - Why should drivers avoid discussing the nature or value of their cargo?
   Reasons:

7. **Regular Inspection:**
   - What should drivers regularly inspect to prevent cargo theft?
   Inspection Points:

Conclusion

Reflecting on Cargo Theft Prevention

1. **Vigilance and Awareness:**
   - How can security personnel and drivers maintain vigilance and awareness to prevent cargo theft?
   Strategies:

2. **Proactive Measures:**
   - What proactive measures can be taken to reduce the risk of cargo theft?
   Measures:

3. **Collaboration:**
   - How can collaboration between different stakeholders enhance cargo theft prevention?
   Collaboration Strategies:

4. **Continuous Learning and Adaptation:**
   - Why is continuous learning and adaptation important in combating cargo theft?
   Importance:

5. **Community and Network:**
   - How can building a network of trust within the supply chain community help prevent cargo theft?
   Benefits:

This workbook is designed to help you internalize and apply the key concepts of cargo theft prevention. Regular practice, reflection, and continuous improvement will ensure that you are well-prepared to handle cargo theft threats effectively.

Chapter 8: Limitations in Use of Force by Security Officers

Worksheet: Limitations in Use of Force by Security Officers

Section 1: Introduction

Understanding the Use of Force

1. **Principles of Necessity, Proportionality, and Reasonableness:**
   - Define these principles and explain their importance in the use of force by security officers.
   Definitions and Importance:

   _____

   _____

2. **Ethical and Legal Considerations:**
   - Why is it important to consider ethical and legal implications when deciding to use force?
   Ethical and Legal Considerations:

   _____

   _____

3. **Scenario Analysis:**
   - Consider a scenario where a security officer encounters an unarmed intruder in a corporate office. What steps should the officer take to resolve the situation?
   Steps to Resolve the Situation:

   _____

   _____

4. **Role of Training:**
   - How does training help security officers handle confrontational situations effectively?
   Role of Training:

   _____

   _____

Section 2: Definitions

Key Terms in Use of Force

1. **Reasonable Force:**
   - What is reasonable force, and provide an example.
   Definition and Example:

   _____

   _____

2. **Excessive Force:**
   - Define excessive force and provide an example of when it might occur.
   Definition and Example:

   _____

   _____

3. **Deadly Force:**
   - What is deadly force, and when is it justified?
   Definition and Justification:

   _____

   _____

4. **Non-Lethal Force:**
   - Describe non-lethal force and provide examples of non-lethal tools.
   Description and Examples:

   _____

   _____

5. **Scenario Application:**
   - Consider a situation where a security officer must use force. Identify which type of force is appropriate and why.
   Situation and Appropriate Force:

   _____

   _____

Section 3: Types of Force

Different Types of Force and Their Applications

1. **Constructive Authority:**
   - Explain constructive authority and its components.
   Explanation:

   _____

   _____

2. **Physical Force:**
   - Describe the use of physical force and provide an example of when it might be used.
   Description and Example:

   _____

   _____

3. **Mechanical Force:**
   - List tools included in mechanical force and describe their appropriate use.
   Tools and Appropriate Use:

   _____

   _____

4. **Chemical Agents:**

- What are chemical agents, and when should they be used?
  Description and Use:

  _____

  _____

5. **Enhanced Mechanical Force:**
   - Define enhanced mechanical force and provide examples.
   Definition and Examples:

   _____

   _____

6. **Firearms (Deadly Force):**
   - When is the use of firearms justified, and what are the legal and ethical considerations?
   Justification and Considerations:

   _____

   _____

   _____

Section 4: Self-Defense

Principles and Practices of Self-Defense

1. **Legal Boundaries:**
   - What are the legal principles governing self-defense for security officers?
   Legal Principles:

   _____

   _____

2. **Reasonable Force in Self-Defense:**
   - Explain the concept of reasonable force in self-defense situations.
   Explanation:

   _____

   _____

3. **Training and Preparedness:**
   - Why is training essential for effective self-defense?
   Importance of Training:

   _____

   _____

4. **Defensive Equipment and Tools:**
   - List and describe the defensive tools commonly used by security officers.
   Tools and Descriptions:

   _____

   _____

5. **Documentation and Reporting:**
   - Why is documentation important in self-defense incidents, and what should it include?

Importance and Inclusions:

_____

_____

6. **Ethical Considerations:**
   o Discuss the ethical considerations in using self-defense as a security officer.
   Ethical Considerations:

   _____

   _____

_____

Section 5: Defense of Others

Responsibilities and Strategies for Defending Others

1. **Assessing the Need for Force:**
   o How do security officers determine if force is necessary to defenc others?
   Assessment Criteria:

   _____

   _____

2. **Proportionality in Defense of Others:**
   o Explain the principle of proportionality in the defense of others.
   Explanation:

   _____

   _____

3. **Scenario Analysis:**
   o Describe a scenario where a security officer must defend someone and the steps taken to ensure proportional force.
   Scenario and Steps:

   _____

   _____

4. **Documentation of Defense Incidents:**
   o What should be included in the documentation of incidents involving the defense of others?
   Documentation Inclusions:

   _____

   _____

_____

Section 6: Warning Shots

Considerations and Alternatives to Warning Shots

1. **Risks of Warning Shots:**

- What are the potential risks associated with firing warning shots?
  Risks:

  _____

  _____

2. **Alternatives to Warning Shots:**
   - What are some effective alternatives to firing warning shots?
     Alternatives:

   _____

   _____

3. **Scenario Analysis:**
   - Consider a scenario where a security officer might be tempted to fire a warning shot. What alternative actions could they take?
     Scenario and Alternatives:

   _____

   _____

_____

Section 7: Defense of Premises or Personal Property

Strategies for Defending Property

1. **Legal Boundaries:**
   - What are the legal boundaries for using force to defend property?
     Legal Boundaries:

   _____

   _____

2. **Non-Violent Methods:**
   - List non-violent methods for protecting property and provide examples.
     Non-Violent Methods:

   _____

   _____

3. **Scenario Analysis:**
   - Describe a scenario where a security officer uses non-violent methods to protect property.
     Scenario:

   _____

   _____

4. **Documentation:**
   - Why is documentation important in incidents involving property defense, and what should it include?
     Importance and Inclusions:

   _____

   _____

<u>Section 8: Scope of Liability</u>

Understanding Liability in Use of Force

1. **Civil and Criminal Liability:**
   - What are the potential civil and criminal liabilities for security officers using force?
   Potential Liabilities:

   _____

2. **Minimizing Liability Risks:**
   - How can security officers minimize liability risks when using force?
   Minimizing Risks:

   _____

3. **Role of Training:**
   - How does regular training help mitigate liability risks?
   Role of Training:

   _____

4. **Case Study Analysis:**
   - Analyze a case study where liability issues arose from the use of force. What lessons can be learned?
   Case Study and Lessons:

   _____

5. **Regular Audits:**
   - Why are regular audits of use-of-force incidents important, and what should they cover?
   Importance and Coverage:

   _____

   _____

<u>Conclusion</u>

Reflecting on the Use of Force

1. **Judicious Use of Force:**
   - Summarize the importance of judicious and responsible use of force.
   Summary:

   _____

   _____

2. **Training and Knowledge:**
   - Highlight the role of continuous training and knowledge in making informed decisions about using force.
     Importance:
     _____

     _____

3. **Ethical and Legal Considerations:**
   - Discuss the importance of adhering to ethical and legal guidelines in the use of force.
     Discussion:
     _____

     _____

4. **Documentation and Accountability:**
   - Explain why proper documentation and accountability are crucial in instances where force is used.
     Explanation:
     _____

     _____

5. **Community and Empathy:**
   - Describe how empathy and understanding can play a role in security work.
     Description:
     _____

     _____

By understanding and applying these principles and practices, security officers can effectively manage situations requiring the use of force while maintaining the highest standards of professionalism and responsibility.

Chapter 9: Incident Command System – Emergency Response

Worksheet: Incident Command System – Emergency Response by Security Officers

Section 1: Introduction

Understanding the Importance of ICS

1. **Why is the Incident Command System (ICS) crucial for emergency response?**
   Importance:
   _____
   _____

2. **Describe a scenario where ICS would be essential.**
   Scenario Description:
   _____
   _____

3. **How does ICS ensure coordinated and efficient emergency response?**
   Coordination and Efficiency:
   _____
   _____

4. **What role does training play in the effective implementation of ICS?**
   Role of Training:
   _____
   _____

   _____

Section 2: What is ICS?

Components and Structure of ICS

1. **List and define the five primary functions of ICS.**
   Command:
   _____
   _____

   Operations:
   _____
   _____

   Planning:
   _____
   _____

   Logistics:
   _____
   _____

Finance/Administration:

_____

_____

2. **Explain the scalability and flexibility of ICS.**
   Scalability and Flexibility:

_____

_____

3. **Describe the concept of Unified Command in ICS.**
   Unified Command:

_____

_____

4. **Why is standardized terminology important in ICS?**
   Importance of Standardized Terminology:

_____

_____

_____

Section 3: History of Incident Command System

Evolution and Development of ICS

1. **What prompted the development of ICS in the 1970s?**
   Development Prompt:

_____

_____

2. **Explain the role of the FIRESCOPE program in the creation of ICS.**
   Role of FIRESCOPE:

_____

_____

3. **How did ICS prove its effectiveness beyond firefighting?**
   Effectiveness Beyond Firefighting:

_____

_____

4. **Discuss the integration of ICS into the National Incident Management System (NIMS).**
   Integration into NIMS:

_____

_____

5. **Provide an example of a major incident where ICS was effectively deployed.**
   Example Incident:

_____

_____

Section 4: Benefits of ICS

Advantages of Implementing ICS

1. **How does ICS enhance interagency coordination?**
   Enhanced Coordination:

   _____

   _____

2. **What benefits does ICS offer in terms of resource management?**
   Resource Management Benefits:

   _____

   _____

3. **Why is clear communication crucial in ICS, and how is it achieved?**
   Clear Communication:

   _____

   _____

4. **Explain the importance of accountability and documentation in ICS.**
   Accountability and Documentation:

   _____

   _____

5. **Give an example of a real-world incident that demonstrates the effectiveness of ICS.**
   Real-World Example:

   _____

   _____

_____

Section 5: Basic Features of ICS

Fundamental Characteristics of ICS

1. **Why is standardization critical in ICS?**
   Critical Nature of Standardization:

   _____

   _____

2. **Describe the modular organization of ICS and its benefits.**
   Modular Organization and Benefits:

   _____

   _____

3. **What does "management by objectives" mean in the context of ICS?**
   Management by Objectives:

   _____

   _____

4. **How does ICS ensure integrated communications among different agencies?**
   Integrated Communications:

   _____

   _____

5. **Explain the principles of unity of command and chain of command in ICS.**
   Unity and Chain of Command:

   _____

   _____

   _____

_____

Section 6: Incident Command and Command Staff Functions

Key Roles in ICS

1. **What are the primary responsibilities of the Incident Commander (IC)?**
   Responsibilities of IC:

   _____

   _____

2. **List and describe the roles of the Command Staff.**
   Public Information Officer (PIO):

   _____

   _____

   Safety Officer (SO):

   _____

   _____

   Liaison Officer (LO):

   _____

   _____

3. **Provide a real-life example of how the Command Staff roles were utilized during an incident.**
   Example:

   _____

   _____

_____

Section 7: General Staff Functions

Operational Management in ICS

1. **What is the primary role of the Operations Section?**
   Role of Operations Section:

   _____

   _____

2. **Explain the responsibilities of the Planning Section.**
   Responsibilities of Planning Section:

   _____

   _____

3. **Describe the tasks managed by the Logistics Section.**
   Tasks of Logistics Section:

   _____

   _____

4. **What financial responsibilities does the Finance/Administration Section handle?**
   Responsibilities of Finance/Administration Section:

   _____

   _____

5. **Provide an example of how these sections work together in a specific incident response.**
   Example:

   _____

   _____

   _____

Section 8: Common Responsibilities

Shared Duties in ICS

1. **Why is it important for all personnel to understand ICS principles and functions?**
   Importance of Understanding ICS:

   _____

   _____

2. **What role does effective communication play in ICS?**
   Role of Effective Communication:

   _____

   _____

3. **How is safety prioritized within ICS?**
   Prioritization of Safety:

   _____

   _____

4. **Explain the importance of resource tracking in ICS.**
   Importance of Resource Tracking:

   _____

   _____

5. **Discuss the significance of thorough documentation in ICS.**
   Significance of Documentation:

   _____

   _____

<u>Conclusion</u>

Reflecting on ICS

1. **Summarize the key takeaways about the Incident Command System (ICS).**
   Key Takeaways:
   _____

   _____

2. **How does ICS ensure effective and responsible incident management?**
   Effective and Responsible Management:
   _____

   _____

3. **Why is it essential for security officers and emergency responders to have a deep understanding of ICS?**
   Essential Understanding:
   _____

   _____

4. **What continuous improvement practices can be applied to enhance ICS implementation?**
   Continuous Improvement Practices:
   _____

   _____

By completing this workbook, security officers and emergency responders can ensure they have a comprehensive understanding of the Incident Command System (ICS), enabling them to effectively manage emergencies and contribute to coordinated, efficient response efforts.

Chapter 10: Document Fraud

Worksheet: Document Fraud by Security Officers

<u>Section 1: Introduction</u>

Understanding Document Fraud

1. **Why is document fraud a significant threat in today's security landscape?**
   Explanation:

   _____

   _____

2. **What are some potential consequences of document fraud?**
   Consequences:

   _____

   _____

3. **How does document fraud impact national security?**
   Impact on National Security:

   _____

   _____

4. **Why is the role of security professionals critical in preventing document fraud?**
   Importance of Security Professionals:

   _____

   _____

5. **Provide a real-world example of the impact of document fraud.**
   Example:

   _____

   _____

<u>Section 2: Security Features</u>

Key Security Features in Genuine Documents

1. **What are holograms and how do they help in preventing document fraud?**
   Holograms:

   _____

   _____

2. **Explain the purpose and effectiveness of watermarks.**
   Watermarks:

   _____

   _____

3. **What is microprinting and why is it a valuable security feature?**
   Microprinting:

   _____

   _____

4. **Describe the role of color-shifting ink in document security.**
   Color-Shifting Ink:

   _____

   _____

5. **How does incorporating biometric data enhance document security?**
   Biometric Data:

   _____

   _____

6. **Why are advanced security features important in modern documents?**
   Importance of Advanced Security Features:

   _____

   _____

   _____

Section 3: Document Examination Process

Steps in Examining Documents for Authenticity

1. **What should be the first step in examining a document for authenticity?**
   First Step:

   _____

   _____

2. **Describe the tactile examination process. What should you be looking for?**
   Tactile Examination:

   _____

   _____

3. **List the technological tools that aid in document examination and explain their uses.**
   Technological Tools:

   _____

   _____

4. **Why is comparative analysis important in the document examination process?**
   Comparative Analysis:

   _____

   _____

5. **Provide an example of how advanced examination processes can detect document fraud.**
   Example:

   _____

   _____

Identifying and Addressing Fake ID Websites

1. **What are some common red flags that indicate a document might be a fake?**
   Red Flags:

   _____

   _____

2. **Why do fake IDs often lack sophistication compared to genuine documents?**
   Lack of Sophistication:

   _____

   _____

3. **Discuss the legal implications of handling incidents involving fake IDs.**
   Legal Implications:

   _____

   _____

4. **How can security professionals stay informed about fake ID websites and their methods?**
   Staying Informed:

   _____

   _____

5. **Provide an example of how a fake ID was identified and what steps were taken.**
   Example:

   _____

   _____

Section 5: Types of Documents Targeted

Commonly Targeted Documents in Document Fraud

1. **Why are passports and visas frequently targeted by fraudsters?**
   Passports and Visas:

   _____

2. **Explain the risks associated with forged driver's licenses and national ID cards.**
   Driver's Licenses and National ID Cards:

   _____

3. **What financial risks are posed by counterfeit bank documents and credit cards?**
   Bank Documents and Credit Cards:

4. **How do fake employment and educational documents impact professional systems?**
   Employment and Educational Documents:

5. **Describe the potential consequences of altered legal and government documents.**
   Legal and Government Documents:

Section 6: Equipment for Detecting Fake IDs

Essential Equipment for Identifying Counterfeit Documents

1. **How does ultraviolet light help in detecting fake IDs?**
   Ultraviolet Light:

2. **What role do magnifiers and microscopes play in document examination?**
   Magnifiers and Microscopes:

3. **Explain how barcode scanners are used to verify IDs.**
   Barcode Scanners:

4. **Describe the importance of RFID readers in document security.**
   RFID Readers:

5. **What are forgery detection kits and how do they assist security professionals?**
   Forgery Detection Kits:

6. **Why is training essential in effectively using these tools?**
   Importance of Training:

<u>Conclusion</u>

Reflecting on Document Fraud Prevention

1. **Summarize the key takeaways from this chapter on document fraud.**
   Key Takeaways:

   _____

   _____

2. **How can security professionals stay vigilant in detecting document fraud?**
   Staying Vigilant:

   _____

   _____

3. **Why is understanding targeted documents important for security officers?**
   Importance of Understanding Targeted Documents:

   _____

   _____

4. **Discuss the benefits of utilizing advanced equipment in document verification.**
   Benefits of Advanced Equipment:

   _____

   _____

5. **What continuous improvement practices can enhance document fraud prevention strategies?**
   Continuous Improvement Practices:

   _____

   _____

> By completing this workbook, security professionals will gain a comprehensive understanding of document fraud, the tools and techniques used to detect and prevent it, and the importance of their role in safeguarding individuals, organizations, and public safety.

Chapter 11: Active Shooter Response Workbook

Worksheet: Active Shooter Response for Security Officers

Section 1: Introduction

Understanding Active Shooter Situations

1. **Describe the importance of preparedness for active shooter situations.**
   Importance of Preparedness:
   _____
   _____

2. **Reflect on the role of security professionals in an active shooter scenario. How can their actions impact the outcome?**
   Role of Security Professionals:
   _____
   _____

3. **Provide a real-world example of an active shooter situation where security personnel played a critical role.**
   Example:
   _____
   _____

4. **What are the psychological and emotional impacts of active shooter situations on survivors and responders?**
   Psychological and Emotional Impacts:
   _____
   _____

5. **Why is effective communication crucial in managing active shooter situations?**
   Importance of Communication:
   _____
   _____

Section 2: Active Shooter Defined

Characteristics and Behaviors of Active Shooters

1. **Define an active shooter and explain their typical behavior patterns.**
   Definition and Behavior Patterns:
   _____

2. **What are the common warning signs that may indicate someone is an active shooter threat?**

Warning Signs:

_____

_____

3. **How does the "Run, Hide, Fight" protocol improve survival rates during active shooter events?**
   Effectiveness of "Run, Hide, Fight":

   _____

   _____

4. **Provide an example of a historical active shooter incident and the response actions taken.**
   Historical Incident and Response:

   _____

   _____

   _____

Section 3: Targets

Common Targets and Security Measures

1. **List and describe the types of locations commonly targeted by active shooters.**
   Common Targets:

   _____

   _____

2. **Why are schools considered high-risk targets for active shooters?**
   Schools as High-Risk Targets:

   _____

   _____

3. **What specific security measures can be implemented in workplaces to prevent active shooter incidents?**
   Workplace Security Measures:

   _____

   _____

4. **Explain the importance of having active shooter response plans in public venues such as shopping centers and entertainment venues.**
   Importance of Response Plans in Public Venues:

   _____

   _____

5. **Provide an example of an active shooter incident in a public venue and discuss the security measures that were or could have been effective.**
   Example and Security Measures:

   _____

   _____

Section 4: What to Expect

Typical Responses and Shooter Behavior

1. **Describe the common reactions of individuals during an active shooter situation.**
   Common Reactions:
   _____
   _____

2. **What behaviors and tactics are typically exhibited by active shooters?**
   Shooter Behaviors and Tactics:
   _____
   _____

3. **How can security professionals manage the chaos and confusion during an active shooter event?**
   Managing Chaos and Confusion:
   _____
   _____

4. **Provide an example of a successful response to an active shooter incident and the factors that contributed to its success.**
   Successful Response Example:
   _____
   _____
   _____

Section 5: Communication

Effective Communication Strategies

1. **Why is internal communication critical during an active shooter incident?**
   Importance of Internal Communication:
   _____
   _____

2. **What information should security personnel provide to law enforcement upon their arrival?**
   Information for Law Enforcement:
   _____
   _____

3. **How should security professionals communicate with building occupants during an active shooter situation?**
   Communication with Occupants:
   _____
   _____

4. **Discuss the role of public information management and the importance of having a designated spokesperson.**

Public Information Management:

_____

_____

_____

Section 6: Assess the Situation

Rapid Assessment and Decision Making

1. **Explain the importance of quickly determining the shooter's location during an active shooter event.**
   Determining Shooter's Location:

   _____

   _____

2. **What factors should be considered when evaluating immediate dangers in an active shooter situation?**
   Evaluating Immediate Dangers:

   _____

   _____

3. **How can security professionals identify and direct people to safe escape routes?**
   Identifying and Directing to Escape Routes:

   _____

   _____

4. **Why is environmental familiarity important for security personnel in active shooter situations?**
   Importance of Environmental Familiarity:

   _____

   _____

Section 7: Response

Executing Response Strategies

1. **What are the key components of the "Run, Hide, Fight" protocol?**
   Components of "Run, Hide, Fight":

   _____

   _____

2. **Describe the steps involved in safely evacuating individuals during an active shooter incident.**
   Steps for Safe Evacuation:

   _____

   _____

3. How can security personnel effectively hide and secure individuals during an active shooter event?
Hiding and Securing Individuals:

_____

_____

4. Explain the importance of defensive actions and how security personnel should be prepared for them.
Importance of Defensive Actions:

_____

_____

5. Provide an example of an active shooter response where the "Run, Hide, Fight" protocol was effectively implemented.
Effective Implementation Example:

_____

_____

_____

Section 8: When Police Arrive

Collaborating with Law Enforcement

1. What should individuals do to remain calm and cooperative when law enforcement arrives during an active shooter situation?
Remaining Calm and Cooperative:

_____

_____

2. Why is it important to keep hands visible and avoid holding objects when law enforcement arrives?
Keeping Hands Visible:

_____

_____

3. What critical information should be provided to law enforcement upon their arrival?
Critical Information for Law Enforcement:

_____

_____

4. Describe the importance of not interfering with law enforcement operations during an active shooter incident.
Avoiding Interference:

_____

_____

5. Provide an example of effective collaboration between security personnel and law enforcement during an active shooter event.
Effective Collaboration Example:

_____

_____

_____

Section 9: Signs of Workplace Violence

Recognizing and Reporting Warning Signs

1. **List and describe behavioral changes that might indicate a potential for workplace violence.**
   Behavioral Changes:

   _____

   _____

2. **What verbal threats should raise concern about potential workplace violence?**
   Verbal Threats:

   _____

   _____

3. **Identify physical actions that might indicate escalating aggression in the workplace.**
   Physical Actions:

   _____

   _____

4. **How can concerning social media posts be used to identify potential threats?**
   Concerning Social Media Posts:

   _____

   _____

5. **Explain the significance of a history of violence in assessing the risk of workplace violence.**
   Significance of History of Violence:

   _____

   _____

6. **Provide an example of early intervention that successfully prevented workplace violence.**
   Early Intervention Example:

   _____

   _____

Section 10: Management Responsibilities

Management's Role in Prevention and Response

1. **What key elements should be included in workplace violence and emergency response policies?**

Key Elements of Policies:

_____

_____

2. **Discuss the importance of regular training and drills for employees.**
   Importance of Training and Drills:

   _____

   _____

3. **How can effective communication systems enhance the response to an active shooter incident?**
   Enhancing Response with Communication Systems:

   _____

   _____

4. **Describe how creating a supportive environment can help in preventing workplace violence.**
   Creating a Supportive Environment:

   _____

   _____

5. **Why is engagement with law enforcement important for active shooter preparedness?**
   Importance of Engagement with Law Enforcement:

   _____

   _____

6. **What role does management play in providing post-incident support?**
   Role in Post-Incident Support:

   _____

   _____

Conclusion

Reflecting on Active Shooter Response

1. **Summarize the key takeaways from this chapter on active shooter response.**
   Key Takeaways:

   _____

   _____

2. **How can security professionals stay vigilant and prepared for active shooter situations?**
   Staying Vigilant and Prepared:

   _____

   _____

3. **Why is collaboration with law enforcement crucial in active shooter scenarios?**
   Importance of Collaboration:

4. **Discuss the importance of continuous learning and adaptation in active shooter preparedness.**

   Continuous Learning and Adaptation:

5. **Provide an example of a successful active shooter response and the key factors that contributed to its success.**

   Successful Response Example:

By completing this workbook, security professionals will gain a comprehensive understanding of active shooter situations, enhancing their ability to respond effectively and protect lives during these critical incidents.

Chapter 12: Suspicious Letters and Packages Awareness

Worksheet: Suspicious Letters and Packages Awareness

Introduction

Understanding the Importance

1. **Why is it crucial for security officers to be aware of suspicious letters and packages?**
   Importance:

   _____

   _____

2. **Reflect on the role security officers play in preventing mail-based threats. How can their actions make a difference?**
   Role and Impact:

   _____

   _____

3. **Provide an example of a historical incident involving suspicious mail and the role of security officers in managing the situation.**
   Historical Example:

   _____

   _____

4. **Discuss how advancements in technology have changed the nature of mail-based threats.**
   Technological Advancements:

   _____

   _____

Section 1: Identifying Suspicious Mail

Recognizing the Signs

1. **List and describe key indicators of suspicious mail.**
   Key Indicators:

   _____

   _____

2. **Why is it important to be cautious with packages from unknown sources or high-risk locations?**
   Importance of Caution:

   _____

   _____

3. **Describe the significance of unusual labeling and physical irregularities in identifying suspicious mail.**

Unusual Labeling and Physical Irregularities:

_____

_____

4. **Provide an example of a suspicious mail scenario and the steps taken to identify it.**

Suspicious Mail Scenario:

_____

_____

_____

Section 2: Initial Response to Suspicious Mail

Immediate Actions and Procedures

1. **What are the first steps to take upon identifying a suspicious letter or package?**

First Steps:

_____

_____

2. **Explain the importance of isolation and evacuation in handling suspicious mail.**

Isolation and Evacuation:

_____

_____

3. **Why is prompt notification to authorities essential when dealing with suspicious mail?**

Prompt Notification:

_____

_____

4. **How should security officers document the discovery and handling of suspicious mail?**

Documentation:

_____

_____

Section 3: Coordination with Emergency Services

Working with Authorities

1. **Discuss the importance of clear communication with emergency services during a suspicious mail incident.**

Clear Communication:

2. **What role does scene preservation play in managing suspicious mail incidents?**
Scene Preservation:

3. **Describe the steps involved in supporting evacuation and medical assistance during such incidents.**
Supporting Evacuation and Medical Assistance:

4. **Provide an example of effective coordination with law enforcement during a suspicious mail incident.**
Effective Coordination Example:

Section 4: Risk Assessment and Management

Evaluating and Mitigating Risks

1. **What factors should be considered when evaluating the threat level of suspicious mail?**
Evaluating Threat Levels:

2. **Explain the importance of understanding different types of mail threats in risk assessment.**
Understanding Types of Threats:

3. **How can security officers make informed decisions regarding evacuation and isolation based on risk assessment?**
Informed Decision-Making:

4. **Why is continuous monitoring and updating of risk assessment protocols essential?**
Continuous Monitoring:

Section 5: Handling Procedures for Suspicious Mail

Safe Handling and Containment

1. **Describe the importance of minimizing handling of suspicious mail items.**
   Minimizing Handling:

2. **What role does personal protective equipment (PPE) play in handling suspicious mail?**
   Role of PPE:

3. **Explain the strategies for containing suspicious mail items safely.**
   Containment Strategies:

4. **Why is maintaining a chain of custody important when handling suspicious mail?**
   Chain of Custody:

Section 6: Training and Preparedness

Ensuring Readiness Through Training

1. **What is the significance of conducting regular drills for handling suspicious mail incidents?**
   Significance of Regular Drills:

2. **How can staying informed about current threat trends enhance preparedness?**
   Staying Informed:

3. **Discuss the benefits of interagency training with law enforcement and emergency responders.**
   Benefits of Interagency Training:

4. **Why is it important to analyze past incidents to improve future responses?**
   Analyzing Past Incidents:

_____

_____

_____

<u>Conclusion</u>

Reflecting on Key Learnings

1. **Summarize the key takeaways from this chapter on suspicious letters and packages awareness.**
   Key Takeaways:

   _____

   _____

2. **How can security officers balance vigilance and normalcy in their daily routines?**
   Balancing Vigilance and Normalcy:

   _____

   _____

3. **Why is it essential to address the psychological well-being of those involved in suspicious mail incidents?**
   Addressing Psychological Well-being:

   _____

   _____

4. **Provide an example of a successful response to a suspicious mail incident and the factors that contributed to its success.**
   Successful Response Example:

   _____

   _____

By completing this workbook, security professionals will enhance their understanding and preparedness for handling suspicious letters and packages, ensuring the safety and security of their environment.

Chapter 13: Technology and Modern Security

Worksheet: Technology and Modern Security

Introduction

Reflect on Technology's Role in Security

1. **In your opinion, why is technology considered a "lifeline" in modern security operations?**
   Response:

   _____

   _____

2. **How does technology bring people together in the context of security? Explain with an example.**
   Response:

   _____

   _____

3. **What are some specific ways that technology can transform a security officer's role from a reactive responder to a proactive guardian?**
   Response:

   _____

   _____

   _____

Section 1: Electronic Physical Security Systems (EPSS)

Exploring the Layers and Customization of EPSS

1. **List and briefly describe the primary components of an EPSS. How does each component contribute to a secure environment?**
   Components and Contributions:

   _____

2. **Think of a specific environment (e.g., hospital, educational institution) and describe how EPSS can be customized to meet its unique security needs.**
   Environment and Customization:

   _____

3. **Describe a scenario in which EPSS would be crucial in responding to an emergency, and explain how it would work to prevent escalation.**
   Emergency Scenario and Response:

4. **What do you see as the primary advantages of integrating multiple security measures within EPSS?**
   Advantages of Integration:

Section 2: CCTV Security Cameras

Understanding the Advantages of Modern CCTV Systems

1. **What features of modern CCTV cameras enhance surveillance? List at least three and explain their impact on security.**
   Enhanced Features and Impact:

2. **Discuss the role of AI in CCTV systems. How does it improve the detection and prevention of security incidents?**
   AI in CCTV:

3. **Give an example of how facial recognition technology in CCTV cameras can help maintain security in high-risk areas.**
   Example of Facial Recognition in High-Risk Areas:

4. **Explain why privacy concerns should be considered when deploying CCTV systems. What practices can help address these concerns?**
   Privacy Concerns and Practices:

Section 3: Security Lighting

Illuminating Security Benefits with Strategic Lighting

1. **Why is security lighting considered an effective deterrent for criminal activity?**
   Security Lighting as a Deterrent:

2. **How does motion-activated lighting improve security in spaces like parking lots?**
   Impact of Motion-Activated Lighting:
   _____
   _____

3. **Describe how security lighting can enhance the effectiveness of other security measures, such as CCTV.**
   Enhanced Effectiveness with Lighting:
   _____
   _____

4. **What considerations should be made to ensure security lighting is effective without causing issues like glare or blind spots?**
   Considerations for Effective Lighting:
   _____
   _____

Section 4: Electric Barbed Wires

Physical and Psychological Barriers for Enhanced Security

1. **Explain how electric barbed wires provide both a physical and psychological deterrent.**
   Physical and Psychological Deterrent:
   _____
   _____

2. **Give an example of a high-security environment where electric barbed wires would be essential, and explain why.**
   High-Security Environment Example:
   _____
   _____

3. **Discuss the importance of maintaining electric barbed wires. What potential risks might arise if maintenance is neglected?**
   Importance of Maintenance:
   _____
   _____

4. **How can electric barbed wires be integrated with other security systems for comprehensive protection?**
   Integration with Other Systems:
   _____
   _____

Securing Access with Biometric Technologies

1. **Briefly describe the process and advantage of each biometric authentication method: Palm Recognition, Iris Recognition, Fingerprint Recognition, and Voice Recognition.**
   Advantages of Each Biometric Method:
   - **Palm Recognition:**
     _____
   - **Iris Recognition:**
     _____
   - **Fingerprint Recognition:**
     _____
   - **Voice Recognition:**
     _____

2. **Provide an example of how iris recognition is used in public security, such as at airports.**
   Example of Iris Recognition:
   _____
   _____

3. **Describe a situation where voice recognition would be particularly useful, especially in maintaining physical distance.**
   Voice Recognition Scenario:
   _____
   _____

4. **What makes biometric authentication a secure form of access control? Discuss the uniqueness and stability of biometric features.**
   Security of Biometric Authentication:
   _____
   _____

Expanding Surveillance with Aerial Technology

1. **List and explain three advantages drones provide for security surveillance and response.**
   Advantages of Drones:
   _____
   _____

2. **How does thermal imaging in drones enhance surveillance in low-visibility conditions?**

Thermal Imaging Benefits:

3. **Describe a scenario where drones would be essential in a large public event, explaining how they enhance situational awareness and crowd safety.**
Drone Scenario for Public Events:

4. **Explain the importance of integrating drones with other security technologies. How does this integration improve response effectiveness?**
Integration with Other Technologies:

Conclusion

Reflecting on Technology's Role in Proactive Security

1. **Summarize the key takeaways from this chapter on modern security technology and its impact on security operations.**
Key Takeaways:

2. **How can security professionals stay updated on new technologies and trends in security? Suggest specific strategies.**
Staying Updated on Technologies:

3. **What are some proactive measures that can be implemented using modern security technology to prevent potential threats?**
Proactive Measures with Technology:

4. **Reflect on how technology supports security professionals in maintaining a safer environment. What benefits and challenges do you foresee in the continued advancement of security technologies?**
Benefits and Challenges:

By completing this workbook, security professionals will gain a deeper understanding of how to leverage technology to safeguard people, assets, and environments effectively.